SOME MAJOR EVENTS IN WORLD WAR II

THE EUROPEAN THEATER

1939 SEPTEMBER—Germany invades Poland; Great Britain, France, Australia, & New Zealand declare war on Germany; Battle of the Atlantic begins. NOVEMBER—Russia invades Finland.

1940 APRIL—Germany invades Denmark & Norway. MAY—Germany invades Belgium, Luxembourg, & The Netherlands; British forces retreat to Dunkirk and escape to England. JUNE—Italy declares war on Britain & France; France surrenders to Germany. JULY—Battle of Britain begins. SEPTEMBER—Italy invades Egypt; Germany, Italy, & Japan form the Axis countries. OCTOBER—Italy invades Greece. NOVEMBER—Battle of Britain over. DECEMBER—Britain attacks Italy in North Africa.

1941 JANUARY—Allies take Tobruk. FEBRUARY—Rommel arrives at Tripoli. APRIL—Germany invades Greece & Yugoslavia. JUNE—Allies are in Syria; Germany invades Russia. JULY—Russia joins Allies. AUGUST—Germans capture Kiev. OCTOBER—Germany reaches Moscow. DECEMBER—Germans retreat from Moscow; Japan attacks Pearl Harbor; United States enters war against Axis nations.

1942 MAY—first British bomber attack on Cologne. JUNE—Germans take Tobruk. SEPTEMBER—Battle of Stalingrad begins. OCTOBER—Battle of El Alamein begins. NOVEMBER—Allies recapture Tobruk; Russians counterattack at Stalingrad.

1943 JANUARY—Allies take Tripoli. FEBRUARY—German troops at Stalingrad surrender. APRIL—revolt of Warsaw Ghetto Jews begins. MAY—German and Italian resistance in North Africa is over; their troops surrender in Tunisia; Warsaw Ghetto revolt is put down by Germany. JULY—allies invade Sicily; Mussolini put in prison. SEPTEMBER—Allies land in Italy; Italians surrender; Germans occupy Rome; Mussolini rescued by Germany. OCTOBER—Allies capture Naples; Italy declares war on Germany. NOVEMBER—Russians recapture Kiev.

1944 JANUARY—Allies land at Anzio. JUNE—Rome falls to Allies; Allies land in Normandy (D-Day). JULY—assassination attempt on Hitler fails. AUGUST—Allies land in southern France. SEPTEMBER—Brussels freed. OCTOBER—Athens liberated. DECEMBER—Battle of the Bulge.

1945 JANUARY—Russians free Warsaw. FEBRUARY—Dresden bombed. APRIL—Americans take Belsen and Buchenwald concentration camps; Russians free Vienna; Russians take over Berlin; Mussolini killed; Hitler commits suicide. MAY—Germany surrenders; Goering captured.

THE PACIFIC THEATER

1940 SEPTEMBER—Japan joins Axis nations Germany & Italy.

1941 APRIL—Russia & Japan sign neutrality pact. DECEMBER—Japanese launch attacks against Pearl Harbor, Hong Kong, the Philippines, & Malaya; United States and Allied nations declare war on Japan; China declares war on Japan, Germany, & Italy; Japan takes over Guam, Wake Island, & Hong Kong; Japan attacks Burma.

1942 JANUARY—Japan takes over Manila; Japan invades Dutch East Indies. FEBRUARY—Japan takes over Singapore; Battle of the Java Sea. APRIL—Japanese overrun Bataan. MAY—Japan takes Mandalay; Allied forces in Philippines surrender to Japan; Japan takes Corregidor; Battle of the Coral Sea. JUNE—Battle of Midway; Japan occupies Aleutian Islands. AUGUST—United States invades Guadalcanal in the Solomon Islands.

1943 FEBRUARY—Guadalcanal taken by U.S. Marines. MARCH—Japanese begin to retreat in China. APRIL—Yamamoto shot down by U.S. Air Force. MAY—U.S. troops take Aleutian Islands back from Japan. JUNE—Allied troops land in New Guinea. NOVEMBER—U.S. Marines invade Bougainville & Tarawa.

1944 FEBRUARY—Truk liberated. JUNE—Saipan attacked by United States. JULY—battle for Guam begins. OCTOBER—U.S. troops invade Philippines; Battle of Leyte Gulf won by Allies.

1945 JANUARY—Luzon taken; Burma Road won back. MARCH—Iwo Jima freed. APRIL—Okinawa attacked by U.S. troops; President Franklin Roosevelt dies; Harry S. Truman becomes president. JUNE—United States takes Okinawa. AUGUST—atomic bomb dropped on Hiroshima; Russia declares war on Japan; atomic bomb dropped on Nagasaki. SEPTEMBER—Japan surrenders.

WORLD AT WAR

MacArthur and the Philippines

WORLD AT WAR

MacArthur and the Philippines

By G. C. Skipper

Consultant:
Professor Robert L. Messer, Ph.D.
Department of History
University of Illinois at Chicago Circle

 CHILDRENS PRESS, CHICAGO

Above: The magazine of the destroyer U.S.S. *Shaw* explodes at Pearl Harbor, Hawaii during the December 7, 1941 attack by Japanese aircraft. A few hours later, the Japanese attacked the Clark Field air base in the Philippines.

JUL 2 8 1992

FRONTISPIECE:
General of the Army Douglas MacArthur

Library of Congress Cataloging in Publication Data

Skipper, G. C.
  MacArthur and the Philippines.

  (World at war)
  Summary: Recounts the history of General MacArthur's obsession with retaking the Philippines from the Japanese, from the Clark Field bombings of 1941 until the destruction of Manila in 1945.
  1. World War, 1939–1945—Campaigns—Philippines—Juvenile literature. 2. MacArthur, Douglas, 1880–1964—Juvenile literature. 3. Philippines—History—Japanese occupation, 1942–1945—Juvenile literature. [1. World War, 1939–1945—Campaigns—Philippines. 2. MacArthur, Douglas, 1880–1964. 3. Philippines—History—Japanese occupation, 1942–1945] I. Title. II. Series: Skipper, G. C. World at war.
  D767.4.S55   940.54′26   81-38520
  ISBN 0-516-04794-9   AACR2

J
940.54
Ski
C. 1

PICTURE CREDITS:
U.S. ARMY PHOTOGRAPH: Cover, pages 4, 9, 14, 18, 21, 24, 28, 32, 33, 37 (top left and bottom), 38 (top left), 41, 42, 44, 45, 46
OFFICIAL U.S. NAVY PHOTOGRAPH: Page 6
NATIONAL ARCHIVES: Pages 13, 35
UPI: Pages 17, 36, 37 (top right and middle), 38 (top right, middle, and bottom)
WIDE WORLD: Page 23
DEFENSE DEPARTMENT PHOTO (MARINE CORPS): Pages 26, 27
LEN MEENTS (Maps): Pages 10, 31

COVER PHOTO:
General Douglas MacArthur and a group of U.S. Army and Philippine officers wade ashore at Leyte Island in the Philippines on October 20, 1944.

PROJECT EDITOR
Joan Downing

CREATIVE DIRECTOR
Margrit Fiddle

The Philippine Islands cover 1,000 miles of the southwest Pacific Ocean, from Mindanao on the south all the way north to Luzon. These islands were yanked into the midst of World War II only a few hours after the Japanese bombed Pearl Harbor in Hawaii.

On December 8, 1941, Japanese Zeros dived screaming at Clark Field, a United States air base on Luzon. American troops there were caught by surprise. Planes were being refueled; some pilots were at briefing sessions and others were at lunch.

The enemy planes roared in and made a low, sweeping pass at the Flying Fortresses on the ground. Japanese bombers unloaded spiraling bombs from 20,000 feet overhead. Machine-gun fire spit angrily from the guns of the Zeros. Then the Japanese aircraft pulled up quickly and disappeared into the clouds.

Several soldiers were killed in the first Clark Field attack, but there was little damage to the American planes on the field.

The Japanese Zeros suddenly came back again, engines roaring. Machine guns barked angrily as the planes once more swept over Clark Field. Men ran in all directions, getting out of the way of the deadly bullets.

The Japanese weren't after the soldiers. They were after the American planes sitting on the ground. This time they did not miss. Clark Field resembled a shooting gallery as the Zeros swept down and across. The machine-gun bullets streaked toward the American planes. The bullets found each target, as did the bombs from high overhead. All over the air base, Flying Fortresses began to explode. They ballooned in a billow of smoke and flame, blowing apart like gasoline cans. The deadly explosions rocked the earth.

Again—suddenly—the Japanese planes were gone. Clark Field was a shambles. All the Flying Fortresses on the field—except three—were destroyed.

This picture of MacArthur (right) and Manuel Quezon, president of the Philippines, was taken some time before the Japanese attack on December 8, 1941.

The war had reached the very doorstep of Douglas MacArthur, Commanding General of the United States Army Forces in the Far East.

MacArthur, who was headquartered in Manila, was a tall man, a soldier in every sense of the word. He had had his first taste of battle in World War I and knew firsthand the discipline necessary to beat the enemy.

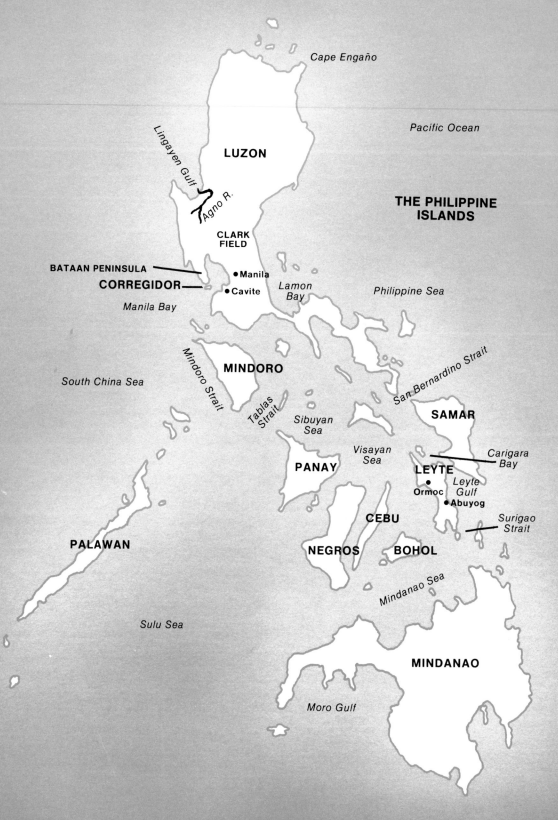

The Clark Field bombing—as well as the news of the Pearl Harbor attack—had sent MacArthur's office into a frenzy of activity. In the midst of the hubbub, MacArthur and one of his staff officers studied a map.

"The Japanese invasion force is bound to follow the Clark Field bombing," MacArthur said. "It makes sense that they'll try to land here." He pointed to Lingayen Gulf on the map.

At that moment, in fact, a huge Japanese invasion force made up of eighty-five transports was pushing through the choppy water toward the Philippines.

The first Japanese troops scrambled ashore on December 22, 1941—at Lingayen Gulf.

Immediately, MacArthur ordered Major General Lewis H. Brereton, commander of the Far East Air Force, to launch his few remaining aircraft.

Even as the American planes roared off to meet the enemy, the Japanese who had landed were cautiously making their way down a highway along the coast—straight toward Manila.

Along the highway MacArthur had set up blockades manned by Filipinos. These Filipinos were poorly trained and had too few guns and too little ammunition. They watched the highway anxiously.

"Look!" shouted one of the Filipinos at the blockade. "Look there!"

The Filipino troops, poorly equipped and virtually untrained, were horrified. Ahead of them, swarming up the highway, were Japanese soldiers. A total of 42,000 Japanese troops had landed. It was the most awful sight the Filipinos had ever seen. Suddenly, sheer panic swept across the blockade. The Filipinos broke and ran. They were not equipped to maintain their positions against the formidable enemy moving toward them.

Japanese General Homma (center) landing on Luzon on December 24, 1941

At MacArthur's headquarters the telephone suddenly rang. Even in the chaos of noise and activity, the clatter of typewriters and the sound of voices, the telephone ring had an immediate, urgent sound to it.

MacArthur removed the corncob pipe from his mouth and laid it carefully down on his desk, careful not to spill the hot tobacco coals.

"General, this is Jonathan," the voice at the other end of the line said. Calling was General Jonathan M. Wainwright, commander of MacArthur's forces in northern Luzon.

"What is it, Jonathan?" asked MacArthur.

"I'd like permission to pull my troops back across the Agno River. We can't hold back the Japanese from here."

"Go ahead," MacArthur told him. He hid the frustration he felt. Things were going very badly.

General MacArthur and General Jonathan Wainwright (on the left) are shown in a picture taken two months before the Japanese attack on Clark Field.

As MacArthur hung up the telephone, he reviewed the situation in his mind. He had not been able to stop the Japanese invasion at the beaches as he had hoped. Now he had no choice but to command his troops to pull back to the Bataan Peninsula.

As night came, a tired MacArthur went to bed. While he slept, twenty-four Japanese transports quietly slipped into Lamon Bay, southeast of Manila. The Japanese formed three columns. The columns, like the tines of a pitchfork, thrust in deadly speed toward Manila.

MacArthur—as he would realize the next morning—was caught in a Japanese pincer that was growing closer and closer together.

MacArthur lost little time. He had to get out of the pincer before it was too late.

"Pull the troops in south Luzon out of there," he commanded. "Tell them to withdraw to Bataan as quickly as possible."

"Sir," one of his staff officers said. MacArthur looked up. "What is it?"

"We should think of leaving Manila, too."

The words cut MacArthur deeply. It was a move he detested, but the staff officer was right. There wasn't much he could do.

"I know," replied MacArthur. "Make arrangements for us to leave tonight. We'll have to move headquarters to Corregidor."

The staff officer glanced at the map. Corregidor Island was at the mouth of Manila Bay, three miles south of the Bataan Peninsula.

"Do you know what tonight is, sir?" asked the officer, turning from the map.

For a moment MacArthur looked puzzled. Then he smiled. "Of course," he said. "It's Christmas Eve."

"Merry Christmas, sir," the officer said. He left the room.

That night MacArthur and his staff, dressed in short-sleeved shirts in the warm night, climbed aboard the *Don Esteban*, a heavy

MacArthur in a typical pose, with dark glasses and corncob pipe

steamer that was idling in an inlet. As the steamer withdrew, MacArthur stood on the deck facing the shoreline. On shore he could see flames licking into the dark sky. The navy yard at Cavite was burning, its oil dumps turning the sky the color of early sunrise.

"They've got the bottle," MacArthur said, "but I've still got the cork." MacArthur meant that whoever held Corregidor controlled Manila Bay. On this night he controlled that island.

The New Year, 1942, did not begin happily for MacArthur. He was settled in his headquarters on Corregidor by then. Word reached him fast. On New Year's Day the Japanese had closed in on Manila. Like the powerful jaws of a dragon, the Japanese forces clamped shut on the city. The American flag was yanked down. Amid wild cheers and shouts, the Japanese ran the Rising Sun up the flagpole. The enemy had captured Manila—and they were determined to conquer the entire Philippines. Not even the great Douglas MacArthur could save the Filipinos now.

Even though MacArthur had left Manila undefended, the Japanese bombed it in December of 1941. This captured Japanese photograph shows a tattered remnant of an American flag amid the wreckage in one section of the city.

MacArthur knew he was at a great disadvantage. Although he pulled back to Bataan nearly 80,000 troops, only 15,000 of these troops were American. The rest—65,000—were Filipinos, and only 10,000 of them were professional soldiers. Most of them were untrained. Equipment was poor and food supplies were short. MacArthur would have to try to make do with what he had.

MacArthur laid out his battle line. Wainwright commanded the western half of Bataan. Brigadier General George M. Parker, Jr. commanded the eastern half.

The Japanese hit on January 13, coming down from the north and slamming into Parker's troops. Within two days of hard fighting, Parker's troops had wiped out two thirds of the Japanese regiment.

MacArthur was elated. He sent encouraging words to the fighting men from his headquarters in Corregidor. His words lifted the spirits of the Filipinos even higher.

On January 16—determined to fight gallantly—the outnumbered Filipinos catapulted themselves into a hard-driving counterattack.

But the Japanese suddenly hit from the east. They poured out of the dense, sticky jungle, screaming, yelling, firing rifles, and slashing at downed troops with bayonets and swords.

The impact of the Japanese attack was too much. The Filipino counterattack collapsed by noon—and a two-mile hole was ripped into MacArthur's defense line.

Things grew even worse. By January 21, Wainwright and his men were in trouble on the western front. They had been cut off when the Japanese forces pushed in from the shore of the South China Sea where they had made amphibious landings.

In the east, Parker's troops had to scramble back in a hasty retreat. The Japanese hit the retreating men from the jungle. Time and again, the enemy pounced on the soldiers, then

Left: American troops on Bataan duck shrapnel from an ammunition dump set on fire during a Japanese bombing raid. Above: General MacArthur and members of his staff at the Bataan front on January 22, 1942.

pulled back into the jungle. The Filipino and American soldiers were exhausted.

Although Filipino and American troops fought with great courage, the war worsened. Food supplies ran out and malaria was rampant. By the end of the first week in March, 5,000 troops had died from malaria alone.

In March of 1942—quite unexpectedly—MacArthur was commanded to leave the Philippines and report to Australia. There he would assume command of all United States forces in the Southwest Pacific. MacArthur protested the orders, but had to obey them. He ordered Wainwright to Corregidor and placed him in charge of all Luzon troops. Later, on March 22, 1942, MacArthur gave Wainwright command of all the Philippines.

MacArthur boarded a PT boat on the night of March 11. For thirty-eight hours the boat traveled through extremely dangerous waters. Japanese ships were all over the place. MacArthur arrived at Mindanao. There, after angrily refusing to board a dilapidated B-17, he boarded a Flying Fortress that had been sent for him and flew to Australia.

A swarm of reporters were waiting for MacArthur when he arrived in Australia. The newsmen shoved and pushed closer to MacArthur's plane.

MacArthur's young son, Arthur, is shown here during the three-month period he spent with his family at his father's headquarters on the island of Corregidor.

MacArthur reached for a used envelope and scribbled down a few words. They were destined to make history.

When he stepped off the plane, MacArthur read the statement to the press: "The president of the United States ordered me to break through the Japanese lines and proceed from Corregidor to Australia for the purpose . . . of organizing the American offensive against Japan, a primary object of which is the relief of the Philippines. I came through and I shall return." After reaching Australia, MacArthur was awarded the Congressional Medal of Honor.

LIFE or DEATH?

TAKE YOUR CHOICE!

U.S.

Surrender notes and propaganda leaflets were dropped by the Japanese over the front lines on Bataan in late January, 1942, two and a half months before the first American and Filipino forces surrendered.

TICKET TO ARMISTICE

USE THIS TICKET, SAVE YOUR LIFE
YOU WILL BE KINDLY TREATED

Follow These Instructions:

1. Come towards our lines waving a white flag.

2. Strap your gun over your left shoulder muzzle down and pointed behined you.

3. Show this ticket to the sentry.

4. Any number of you may surrender with this one ticket.

JAPANESE ARMY HEADQUARTERS

投 降 票

此ノ票ヲ持ツモノハ投降者ナリ
投降者ヲ殺害スルヲ厳禁ス

大 日 本 軍 司 令 官

Sing your way to Peace pray for Peace

Meanwhile, things rapidly deteriorated in the Philippines. On April 2, 1942, the Japanese launched a massive attack on Bataan, forcing American and Filipino troops to pull back and form a second defense line.

The Japanese bombed groves of bamboo that stretched for more than two miles. Fires sprang up and many soldiers were trapped and burned to death. On the night of April 8, 75,000 American and Filippino forces on Bataan—without Wainwright's knowledge—surrendered to the enemy. The Japanese forced these troops to march to prison camps about eighty-five miles up the peninsula. Along the way, about 25,000 Filipino civilians—believing that the Japanese would set them free—joined the march. The gruesome march lasted three days.

Japanese soldiers beat the marchers—already weak from malaria and lack of food—with bamboo poles and clubs. Some marchers who dropped from sheer exhaustion were killed with bayonets. An American captain was buried alive. Others, for no reason at all, were beaten to death.

This became known as the Bataan Death March. More men died in these three days—between 3,000 and 10,000 American troops alone—than died during the previous three months of fighting in Bataan.

Japanese soldiers guard American and Filipino prisoners during the grueling Bataan Death March to Cabana Tuan prison camp.

These Death March prisoners, although weak from malaria and lack of food, had their hands tied behind their backs and were guarded carefully.

These captured Japanese photographs show General Jonathan Wainwright broadcasting the announcement of the surrender of Corregidor on May 8, 1942 and United States troops surrendering to Japanese forces on Corregidor.

The prisoners who did survive the Death March were deliberately starved by the Japanese. Medication was withheld and, to stay alive, the prisoners ate whatever they could get, including mice and garbage. The heroic endurance and the courageous determination of these men to live—and to defeat the enemy—lifted American morale during that disheartening spring of 1942. More than ever, the Americans were determined to defeat the brutal Japanese.

By May 6, Wainwright was forced to surrender his armies. He himself became a prisoner of the Japanese for the duration of the action.

The Japanese, by threatening to murder every person in the garrison, forced Wainwright to broadcast a message to all other troops in the Philippines ordering them to surrender. That broadcast took place on May 8.

As the bad news filtered back to MacArthur, he became more determined than ever to free the Philippines. "I shall return," he had told the world, and he meant to do precisely that.

This unauthorized promise, however, was not part of the American war plan. Other American military leaders favored attacking Formosa and, thus, bypassing the Philippines.

To keep this from happening, MacArthur had to lobby hard in favor of his plan. It took MacArthur two years to convince other military leaders to invade the Philippines again.

The plan MacArthur favored called for the United States to take Eastern New Guinea first, force its way along the northern coast to Sarmi, and then land on Biak, an island two hundred miles northwest of New Guinea.

Between December of 1943 and May of 1944, MacArthur did exactly that. On May 27, his forces landed at Biak. It took the troops a month to secure the area for use as an air base.

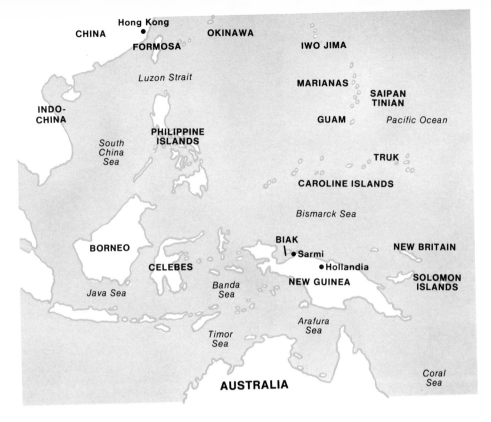

From there, invasion forces under MacArthur's command headed for the Philippines. These forces included Lieutenant General Walter Krueger's Sixth Army, Lieutenant General George C. Kenney's Fifth Air Force, and Admiral Thomas C. Kinkaid's Seventh Fleet. Also steaming toward the Philippines was Admiral Chester W. Nimitz's Third Fleet under Admiral William F. (Bull) Halsey.

Bypassing Mindanao, the invasion forces converged at Leyte Gulf, on the east coast of Leyte. It was October 20, 1944.

On October 20, 1944, the day of the invasion, these troops were pinned down on a Leyte beach by Japanese mortar and machine-gun fire.

MacArthur's Sixth Army assault troops heard the order, "Hit the beaches!" Though sniper fire erupted from the nearby jungle, there was very little opposition to the landings.

MacArthur, who watched the initial fighting from the cruiser *Nashville*, came back on deck about two o'clock. He was a dashing figure. A fresh uniform replaced the one he had been

wearing all day. He was wearing sunglasses.
An old pistol was shoved into his back pocket
and he was smoking his corncob pipe.
MacArthur climbed from the ship into a barge
that carried him to a transport, the *John Land*.
He went ashore with Sergio Osmeña, president
of the Philippines.

MacArthur and the others stepped out of the
boat into water that came up to their knees.
MacArthur waded through the water. On the
beach ahead of him he could see the scattered
remnants of the invasion. As he stepped onto
the sandy beach, someone handed him a
microphone. Once more, his words would be
recorded in the history of World War II. The
broadcast was heard all over the Philippines.

President Sergio Osmeña
and General Douglas
MacArthur head for the
shore to inspect the Leyte
Island beachhead on the
afternoon of October 20.

MacArthur said, "People of the Philippines, I have returned. By the grace of Almighty God our forces stand again on Philippine soil. . . ."

Although MacArthur had returned, the Japanese were not about to let the Americans stay in the Philippines without a fight. They planned to have their navy destroy the hundreds of American ships anchored in Leyte Gulf.

Japanese ships sailed toward Leyte on October 22, two days after the Americans had landed there. The crucial Battle of Leyte Gulf was about to begin.

For three days the battle raged. The Americans attacked the Japanese fleet with everything they had. Two American submarines inflicted the first damage. On the morning of October 23, they caught the main Japanese strike force in the western Philippines. Their torpedoes sank two Japanese ships and badly damaged another. Attack planes from American carriers torpedoed and

The Japanese aircraft carrier *Zuiho* is shown here just before she was torpedoed and sunk during the Battle of Leyte Gulf.

bombed other ships of the Japanese fleet. And American PT boats, battleships, and cruisers destroyed the one Japanese strike force that managed to make it all the way to Leyte Gulf.

The Japanese fought back. They destroyed three American carriers and three destroyers. And they subjected the Americans to the horror of Japanese kamikaze (suicide) planes for the first time. But the Japanese had lost three battleships, four aircraft carriers, ten cruisers, and nine destroyers.

Light tanks head for the front from this Leyte beach to
clear a path for the invading, advancing American troops.

In this greatest sea battle of World War II,
the Americans crushed the Japanese navy. It
would no longer be a force in the war.

By November 2, the Americans had reached
Carigara Bay on the north coast of Leyte and
Abuyog, halfway down the east coast. They
took control of five enemy airfields.

Two corps from Krueger's Sixth Army
fought their way westward. They planned to
converge at Ormoc, on the west coast of Leyte.
Ormoc was the port city used by the Japanese
as headquarters.

Even though the American flag once again was flown in the Philippines (above), the advancing troops made slower progress in Leyte than expected. Jungle swamps (left) and lurking Japanese snipers made the fighting unusually hazardous.
Top left: Fighting a fire on White Beach.
Below: Troops fire at the Japanese-held town of Dulag.

Above: A Japanese prisoner captured near Ormoc is led from his hiding place by American infantrymen.
Top right: This Japanese tank was knocked out during the fighting in the Ormoc area.

Above: A landing ship loaded with troops, supplies, and fighting equipment heads for the Philippines.
Left: This Leyte cathedral served as both a house of worship and a hospital for American wounded.

On December 7, a division of support troops landed just south of Ormoc. They soon linked up with the two corps coming from the west. By Christmas, the fierce battle was all but over. Except for a few isolated pockets of determined Japanese, Leyte had fallen to the Americans.

On December 15, 1944, MacArthur's forces swarmed onto Mindoro, an island south of Luzon. For the next three weeks, during constant attacks by kamikaze pilots, the Americans built airstrips. Planes from these airstrips would be used to cover the major invasion of Luzon.

As it steamed toward Luzon in the early days of January 1945, the American invasion fleet was attacked again and again by kamikaze pilots. But most of the ships kept moving.

On January 9, the fleet arrived in Lingayen Gulf. Nearly 70,000 Sixth Army troops went ashore. They were only 110 miles north of the capital city of Manila. It took them until the end of the month to reach and capture Clark Field, the air base north of Manila. Along the way, the Americans had fought determined Japanese troops who attacked from caves and tunnels well-protected by machine guns and mortars.

On January 29, American troops stormed ashore just north of the Bataan Peninsula. By February 15, they had put down the last of the enemy resistance on Bataan. The peninsula was sealed off.

On February 16, the Americans attacked Corregidor, the island so valiantly defended by Wainwright in 1942. Paratroopers dropped on the island and infantry troops landed. The initial assault met little resistance, but the Japanese were dug in securely. More than 5,000 Japanese troops infested the tunnels that had been dug in Malinta Hill by the Americans in 1942. Also in those tunnels were tons of munitions. In six days of fighting, the

These paratroopers landed on Corregidor on February 16, 1945.
Ten days later, the island fell to the Americans.

Americans cleared much of Corregidor. But
more than 2,000 Japanese still held Malinta
Hill. On February 21, the Japanese set off
some of their blasting powder. They hoped to
dislodge the Americans on top of the hill.
Instead, the resulting explosion killed many of
the Japanese in the hill. Finally, five days later,
another explosion rocked the hill. The battle
for Corregidor was over.

The city of Manila was battered to rubble during the month it took the
American forces to recapture the city from the defending Japanese.
Above: GIs fire on Japanese positions in the Intramuros section.
Below left: Medics bring a battle casualty over the debris-covered
grounds near a ruined university building.
Below right: A flame thrower is used to clean out remaining Japanese
troops who are holed up in a room in the old wall of Intramuros.

Meanwhile, the Americans were closing in on Manila. On February 3, a rescue force of 1,400 men reached Santo Tomás University, which the Japanese were using as a prison camp. The Americans freed most of the four thousand Allied civilians who had been held captive for three years.

The main body of American troops entered the city on February 4—and met 20,000 Japanese defenders who were determined to fight to the death.

The Japanese blew up the military installations in the port and a number of other critical areas. The city was soon in flames, and the fires raged until February 7.

The Japanese holed up in many government buildings and in an old walled section of the city called Intramuros. They fought furiously to defend their positions. The Americans had to fight from building to building, lobbing grenades through windows and falling down flat as the explosions came. Shelling and

On February 23, the Japanese released about three thousand hostages from the old walled city of Intramuros. The Catholic nun shown above was aided in her flight by another evacuee and an American soldier.

mortar fire rocked the city. And during the fighting, the Americans were aware that four thousand Filipino civilians were being held hostage in Intramuros. The Japanese refused to release them. Other civilians in the city searched frantically for a way to escape the fighting. Many were killed.

Finally, after a month of grueling fighting, the Americans took Manila. The city was in ruins, but on March 4, 1945, Manila once again belonged to the Allies.

By the middle of March, the ports in Manila and the landing strips at Clark Field were

General Douglas MacArthur watches infantrymen raise an American flag to signal recapture of the Manila Hotel, where MacArthur lived before his departure to Corregidor in 1942.

being used by United States ships and planes as staging areas on the way to Japan.

Victory was in their grasp, but the Americans had much work left to do in the Philippines. Before Manila fell, they had begun their sweep of the southern islands, but it was not until the end of June that all but a few pockets of Japanese resistance had been knocked out.

The Allies had reconquered the Philippines and MacArthur's promise had been kept.

World War II was coming to an end. Peace was in sight.

Douglas MacArthur embraces an emaciated Jonathan Wainwright
during their first meeting since Wainwright's release from the
Japanese prison camp where he had been held for three years.

INDEX

Page numbers in boldface type indicate illustrations

About the Author

A native of Alabama, G. C. Skipper has traveled throughout the world, including Jamaica, Haiti, India, Argentina, the Bahamas, and Mexico. He has written several other children's books as well as an adult novel. Mr. Skipper has also published numerous articles in national magazines. He is now working on his second adult novel. Mr. Skipper and his family live in Glenside, Pennsylvania, a suburb of Philadelphia.